GLOSSAHOUSE

GlossaHouse.com

Founded in 2012, the GlossaHouse vision is to publish innovative language resources for the global community. As you peruse this catalog, you will encounter a wide range of tools that help students and researchers with language acquisition, especially biblical languages. GlossaHouse values resources that push the boundaries of pedagogy, bringing cutting-edge language learning methods into the biblical language classroom or personal study.

GlossaHouse publications are creative, visually inviting, and refreshingly accessible. Designed for the global community, GlossaHouse resources find their home in classrooms well beyond a North American context, with content ranging from the acquisition of biblical Greek and Hebrew to the preservation of endangered languages.

GlossaHouse gladly entertains new project proposals. If you have a project or a proposal and are searching for a publishing outlet, please consider GlossaHouse. Visit our site at GlossaHouse.com and follow the "Proposals" link for instructions. We look forward to hearing from you and to the opportunity of working with others who share our vision: "Language Resources for the Global Community."

Grace and Peace to you,

Dr. Fredrick J. Long
& Dr. T. Michael W. Halcomb

- Co-Founders -

T. Michael W. Halcomb, PhD

Co-Founder
Acquisitions Editor
Marketing Team
Podcast Lead

Fredriick J. Long, PhD

Co-Founder
Lead Editor
Finance Lead
Podcast Team

Andrew Coutras, PhD

Book Production Manager
Editor

Aubrey de Carvalho

Marketing Lead

Lydia Halcomb

Order Processor
Customer Service
Marketing Team

GlossaHouse.com

TABLE OF CONTENTS

facebook.com/GlossaHouse   @glossahouse   @glossahouse   anchor.fm/glossahouse

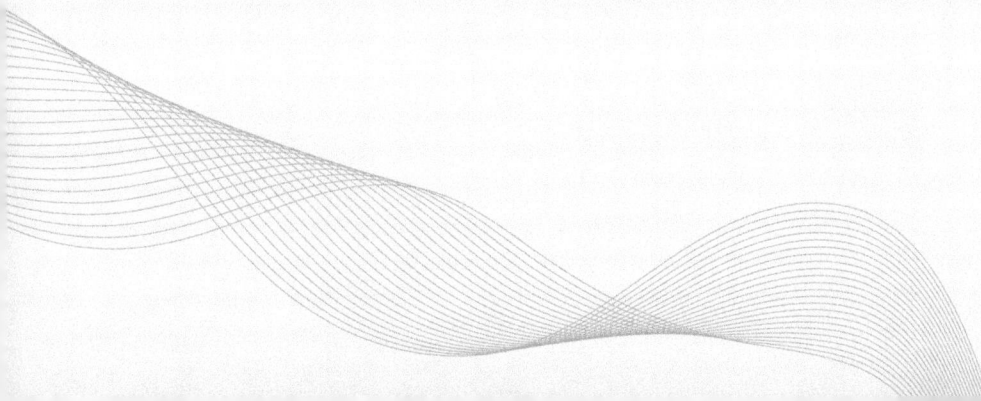

AGROS

PB: $11.99
A: $7.99
App: $9.99

PB: $19.99
App: $9.99

PB: $25.99
A: $9.99
App: $9.99

PB: $21.99
A: $9.99
App: $9.99

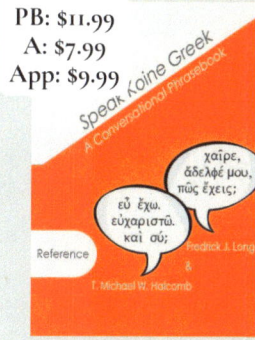

Speak Koine Greek

Contains over 240 sayings, phrases, and idioms in ancient Greek, arranged to help readers build language skills and practice conversation.

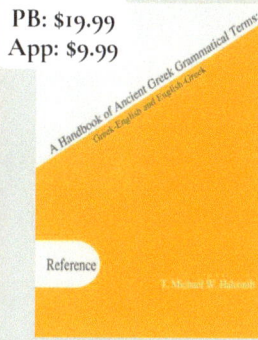

Greek Grammar Terms

Provides learners with a guide to ancient Greek grammatical terms and assists learners in building their grammatical vocabulary.

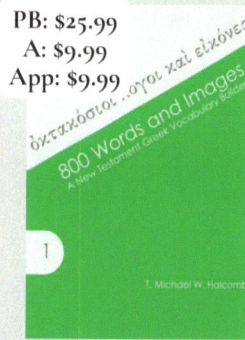

Greek Vocab Builder

Enables learners to comprehend, easily navigate, and recall vocabulary to gain competency and fluency in Koine Greek.

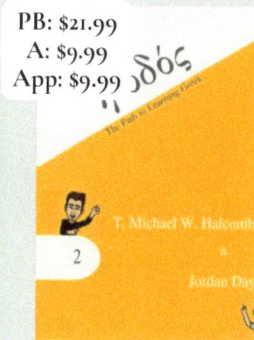

The Path to Learning Greek

Illustrated vocabulary guide meant to help students on their journey toward learning and becoming fluent in Koine Greek.

GlossaHouse.com

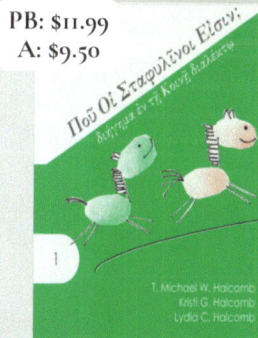

PB: $11.99
A: $9.50

PB: $22.99
V: $39.99

$22.99

$19.99

A Children's Story in Greek

This children's story, told in Koine Greek, is meant to improve students' reading and vocabulary acquisition in ancient Greek.

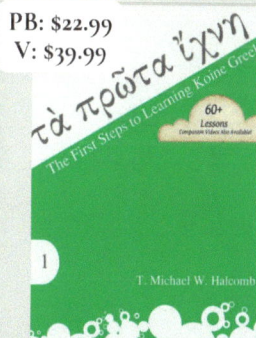

First Steps to Greek Learning

A workbook loaded with fun activities and lessons for students of all ages who want to learn Koine Greek.

Short Stories in Koine Greek

This book contains translations of three of Beatrix Potter's beloved children's books into New Testament Greek.

Max and Mortiz In Koine Greek

This volume consists of a Greek translation using words, phrases, and idioms to tell Wilhelm Busch's story of Max and Mortiz.

PB: $35.99
A: $9.98   Γραμματική
             Greek Grammar

A Beginning-Intermediate Greek
Exegetical and Pragmatic Handbook

-3

Fredrick J. Long

$17.99   Workbook
         for
         Koine Greek Grammar:
         A Beginning-Intermediate
         Exegetical and Pragmatic Handbook

1-3

Fredrick J. Long

$18.99   wer Key & Guide
         for
         the Workbook of
         Koine Greek Grammar: A Beginning-Intermediate
         Exegetical and Pragmatic Handbook

1-3

Fredrick J. Long

$25.99   k and Answer Key & Guide
         for
         Koine Greek Grammar: A Beginning-Intermediate
         Greek Exegetical and Pragmatic Handbook

1-3

Fredrick J. Long

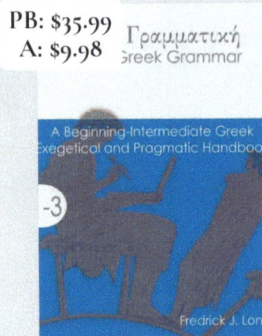

Koine Greek Grammar

This carefully crafted volume, in addition to a full appendix, contains a vocabulary of words used 20+ times, directly taken from Scripture.

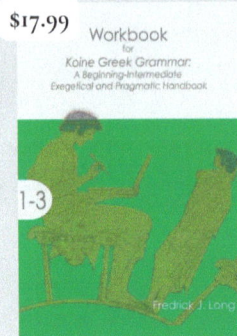

Workbook for K.G.G

This Workbook provides extensive exercises for K.G.G and contains reading & sentence drills drawn from the Greek New Testament.

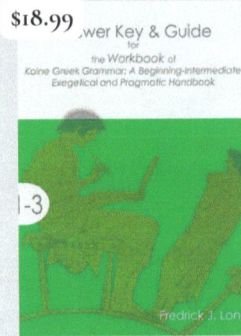

Answer Key & for K.G.G Workbook

This Answer Key & Guide supplements the Workbook of Koine Greek Grammar, providing answers and further guidance for its exercises if needed.

Workbook, Key, & Guide for K.G.G

This volume provides the Koine Greek Grammar Workbook, the Workbook's Answer Key & Guide, and the Workbook's appendices.

GH

GlossaHouse.com

NEW TESTAMENT GREEK SENTENCE DIAGRAMS

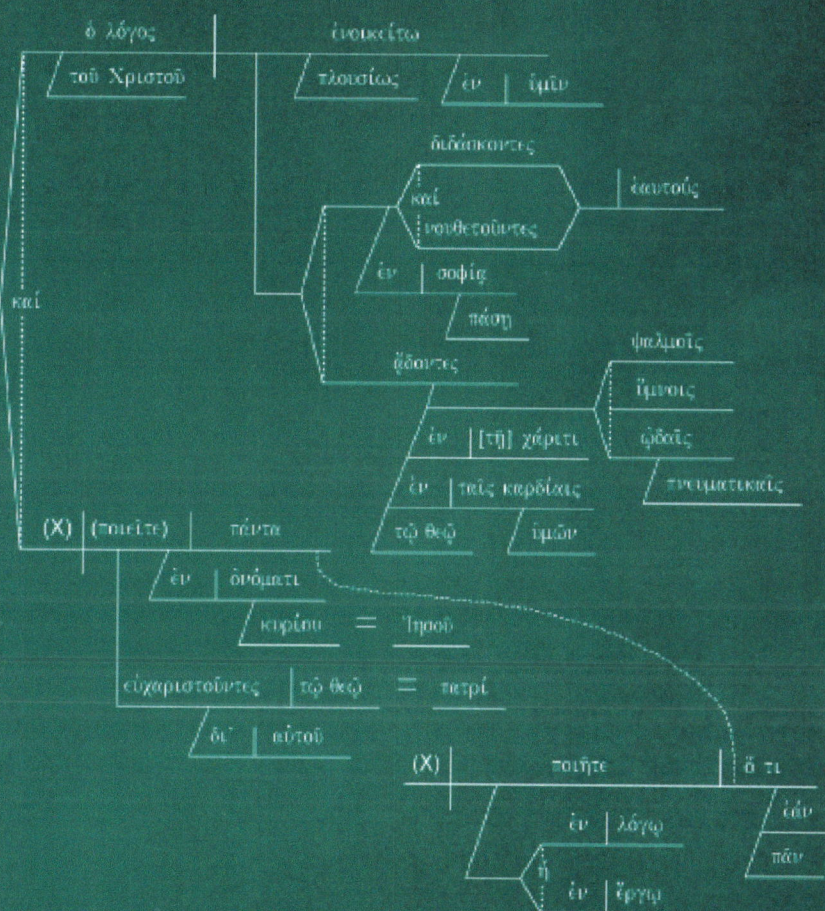

New Testament Greek Sentence Diagrams presents the entire Nestle-Aland 28th edition of the Greek New Testament text in sentence-diagram form, accompanied by approximately 1,000 grammatical notes offering explanations of difficult constructions, alternative diagramming possibilities, etc. This work is useful, giving a detailed grammatical analysis often omitted from commentaries for pastors and teachers looking for exegetical help with difficult grammatical constructions. It also makes it easier for teachers and students looking for pedagogical methods to support the learning of Greek grammar.

New Testament Greek Sentence Diagrams

Randy A. Leedy

Welcome to Koine: Volume 1, Level 1

In this first volume, students will learn the alphabet, numbers, common greetings, simple conversational elements, and more!

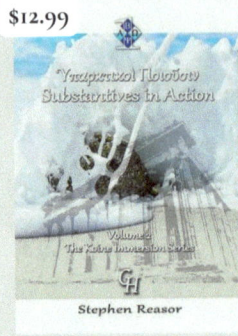

$12.99

Substantives: Volume 2, Level 1

Throughout this second Immersion Series book, students learn lexical and formational entries & cases of both common nouns and verbs.

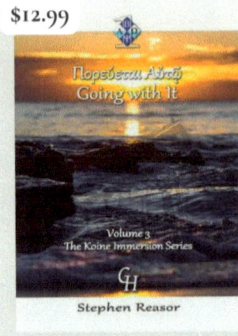

$12.99

Going With It: Volume 3, Level 1

In this third volume, students will learn the genitive and dative substantives, articles, & pronouns, as well as useful vocab words.

$12.99

Koine Immersion Series (Vols. 1-3)

This bundle contains Level 1 books of the Koine Immersion Series (books 1-3). In these, students learn the basics of Greek sentence forms and structures.

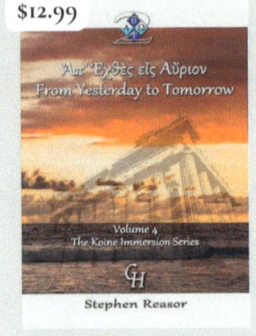

$29.99

Past to Future: Volume 4, Level 2

In this volume, readers learn the forms and functions of the future and aorist tenses. They will also learn words relating to time, seasons, and weather.

$12.99

GlossaHouse.com

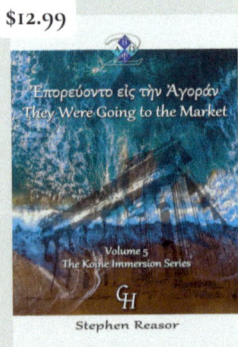

Went to the Market: Volume 5, Level 2

Students learn the forms and functions of imperfect verbs, vocabulary words, and the passive forms of future and aorist verbs.

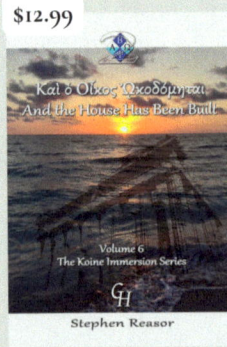

$12.99

A House Built: Volume 6, Level 2

This book helps students learn conjunctions and the forms and functions of perfect and pluperfect verbs.

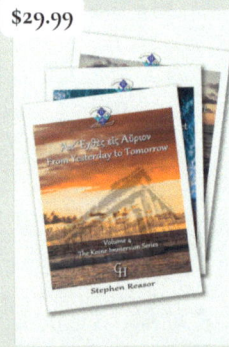

$12.99

Koine Immersion Series (Vols. 4-6)

This bundle contains Level 2 books of the Koine Immersion Series (books 4-6), where readers learn vocabulary & advanced verb forms.

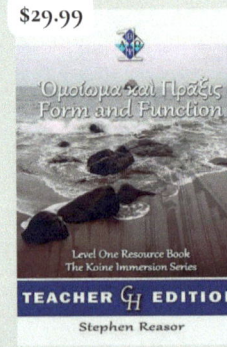

$29.99

Form & Function: Teacher's Edition

This is the Teacher's Edition of the award-winning Koine Immersion Series for Level 1 that includes ebook volumes 1-3.

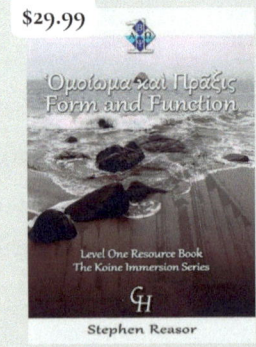

$29.99

Form & Function: Student Resource

This resource explores grammar and syntax of Koine Greek, It also contains ebook volumes 1-3 of the Immersion Series.

$29.99

$9.99

$9.99

$29.99

Ἐπορεύοντο εἰς τὴν Ἀγοράν
They Were Going to the Market

Volume 5
The Koine Immersion Series

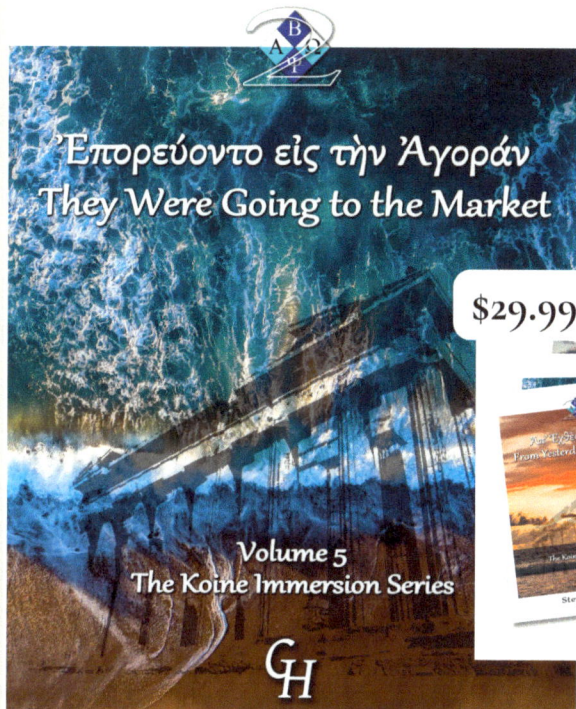

Stephen Reasor

Καὶ ὁ Οἶκος Ὠικοδόμηται
And the House Has Been Built

Volume 6
The Koine Immersion Series

Stephen Reasor

KOINE IMMERSION VOL. 5: GOING TO THE MARKET

In volume five of the Koine Immersion Series, students learn the forms and functions of imperfect verbs, and the passive forms of future and aorist verbs. Vocabulary items include words occurring 85 times or more in the NT as well as words describing food and the marketplace. Available for purchase alone and in the Level 2 Bundle.

KOINE IMMERSION VOL. 6: A HOUSE HAS BEEN BUILT

In volume six of the Koine Immersion Series, students learn conjunctions and the forms & functions of perfect and pluperfect verbs. Vocabulary items include words occurring 70 or more times in the NT as well as words describing buildings, structures, and rooms. Available for purchase alone and in Level 2 Bundle.

GlossaHouse.com

PROVETEXT
EXPLORING SCRIPTURE

GREEK READERS

$34.99

Apostolic Fathers
Greek Reader
The Complete Edition

Apostolic Fathers Greek Reader | Volume 6

4

Editors
Jacob N. Cerone, Shawn J. Wilhite

$19.99 μὴν τοῦ Ἑρμᾶ

The Shepherd
of Hermas

Apostolic Fathers Greek Reader | Volume 5

4

Editors
Jacob N. Cerone, Shawn J. Wilhite

$10.99

ΕΠΙΣΤΟΛΑΙ ΙΓΝΑΤΙΟΥ
The Letters of Ignatius

Apostolic Fathers Greek Reader | Volume 1

4

Edited by Shawn J. Wilhite
& Brian Renshaw

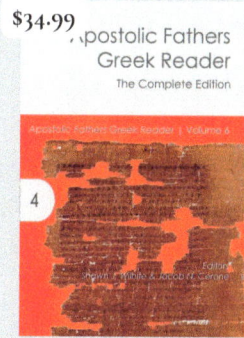

Complete Edition: Apostolic Fathers

This volume offers the complete Greek text of the Apostolic Fathers. Readers will learn about the context, piety, and theology of these early Christian texts.

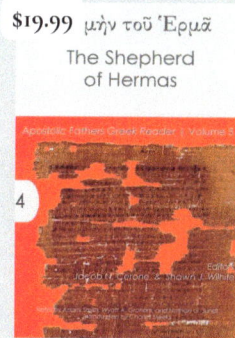

Shepherd of Hermas

Readers will engage in Greek texts of *The Shepherd of Hermas*. Vocabulary words, an introduction, and select bibliography are provided.

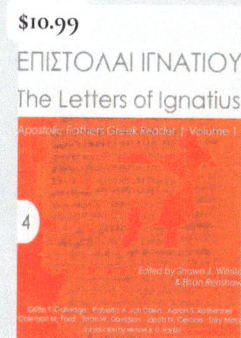

Letters of Ignatius

Scholars will be afforded the Greek text of the *Letters of Ignatius* and learn more about the life and setting of the writings of Ignatius.

GlossaHouse.com

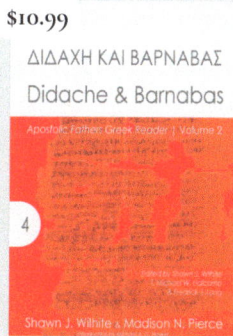

$10.99

ΔΙΔΑΧΗ ΚΑΙ ΒΑΡΝΑΒΑΣ
Didache & Barnabas

Apostolic Fathers Greek Reader | Volume 2

4

Shawn J. Wilhite & Madison N. Pierce

$13.99 ιαρπος, Παπίας,
καὶ Διόγνητος

Polycarp, Papias,
and Diognetus

Apostolic Fathers Greek Reader | Volume 3

4

Editors
Jacob N. Cerone,
Shawn J. Wilhite

$14.99 Ἡ ΚΑΙ ΔΕΥΤΕΡΗ
ΕΠΙΣΤΟΛΑΙ ΚΛΗΜΕΝΤΙΟΥ

1 & 2 Clement

Apostolic Fathers Greek Reader | Volume 4

4

Jacob N. Cerone,
Justin Anderson

Didache and Barnabas

This volume assists students in reading the Greek texts of *Didache* (Shawn J. Wilhite) and *Barnabas* (Madison N. Pierce).

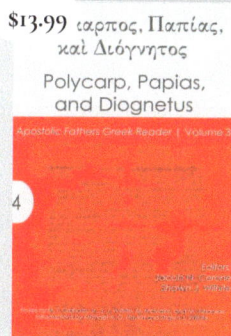

Polycarp, Papias, and Diognetus

Readers will engage the Greek texts of *Polycarp's Epistle to the Philippians*, *Martyrdom of Polycarp*, *Papias*, and *Diognetus*.

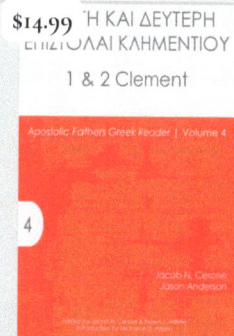

1 & 2 Clement

This ideal resource, created for students of early Christianity, focuses on the Greek texts of *1 Clement* and *2 Clement*.

$19.99

IAKΩBOY

James: A Beginning-Intermediate
Greek Reader

3

Darian Lockett & Wes Lynd

$12.99

IΩANNOY A B Γ

1-3 John
A General Reader

3

Edited by
J. Klay Harrison and Chad M. Foster

$12.99

ΠΡΟΣ ΚΟΛΟΣΣΑΕΙΣ
ΠΡΟΣ ΦΙΛΗΜΟΝΑ

Colossians-Philemon
A Beginning-Intermediate Greek Reader

3

Roy R. Jeal

$14.99

Dio Chrysostom's
Kingship Oration 1

An Advanced Greek Reader
with a New Translation

Fredrick J. Long & J. R. Wright, eds.

with contributions by Garrett Best, Jerry D. Breen,
Esteban Hidalgo, Rico Koch, Matthew R. Peterson,
Kevin M. Southerland, and Jordan C. Stanley

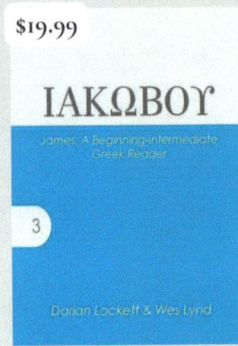

James: A Greek Reader

1-3 John: A Greek Reader

Colossians & Philemon in Koine

Dio Chrysostom's Kingship Oration 1

A Tier 3 resource designed to build confidence in understanding Greek and to encourage the reading of the Greek New Testament.

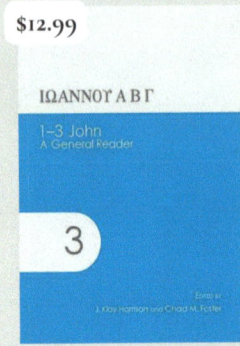

The goal of this book is to give any user the ability to exercise and extend their beginning Greek education & read directly from the Greek New Testament.

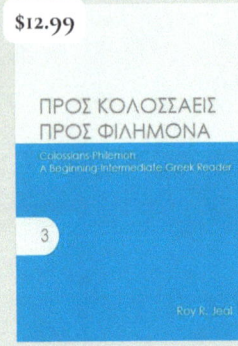

This resource gives vocabulary glosses, explanations, and translational helps for the students wanting to grow in their Koine Greek.

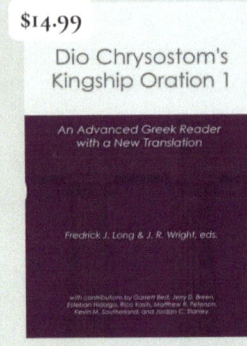

This self-study resource provides space for composing one's own Greek translation with an English version given for comparison.

GlossaHouse.com

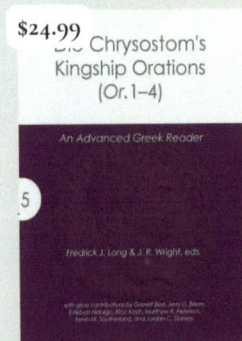

$24.99

Dio Chrysostom's
Kingship Orations
(Or. 1-4)

An Advanced Greek Reader

5

Fredrick J. Long & J. R. Wright, eds.

with gloss contributions by Garrett Best, Jerry D. Breen,
Esteban Hidalgo, Rico Koch, Matthew R. Peterson,
Kevin M. Southerland, and Jordan C. Stanley

$14.99

The Life of Adam
and Eve and The
Testament of Adam

An Advanced Greek Reader

5

Jacob N. Cerone

$19.99

1-4 Baruch

An Advanced Greek Reader
with a Translation

J. R. Wright

$12.99

Lives
of the Prophets

An Advanced Greek Reader

5

Marc Grønbech-Dam

Dio Chrysostom's Kingship Or. 1-4

Life of Adam & Eve: Greek Reader

1-4 Baruch: A Greek Reader

Lives of Prophets: Greek Reader

This ideal volume provides and explains the first four of the collection Kingship Orations, written for King Tarajan.

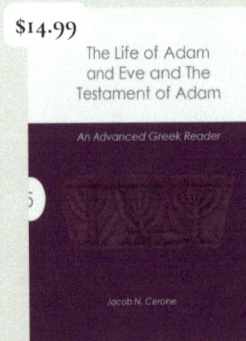

This advanced reader contains an introduction for & the Greek texts of Jewish Apocryphal works as well as helpful glosses.

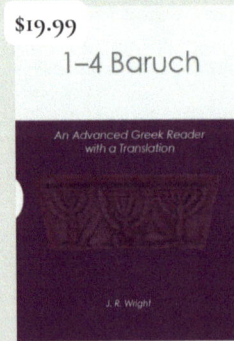

This book, as an advanced Greek reader, has prepared footnotes with glosses, translation helps, and morphological helps.

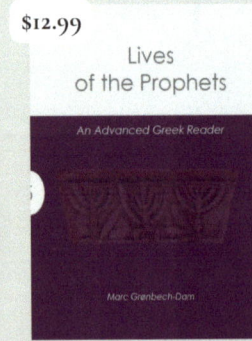

This particular JTGR volume contains an introduction & the Greek text of the Jewish Apocryphal work *Lives of the Prophets*.

ROMANS: A GREEK READER

This new release is a Tier 3 GlossaHouse resource in the Accessible Greek Resources and Online Studies (AGROS) series. These Tier 3 resources are designed to build confidence in understanding Greek and to encourage the reading of the Greek New Testament by providing vocabulary glosses, morphological explanations, and translations helps. Any student who uses this book will be able to read directly from the Greek New Testament, exercise his or her beginning Greek learning, and see how grammatical and syntactical classifications affect meaning and translation in context.

GlossaHouse.com

$19.99

ΠΡΟΣ ΡΩΜΑΙΟΥΣ

Romans: A Beginning-Intermediate Greek Reader

3

Adam W. Jones & Carmen A. Pilant

$19.99

1–4 Baruch

An Advanced Greek Reader
with a Translation

5

J. R. Wright

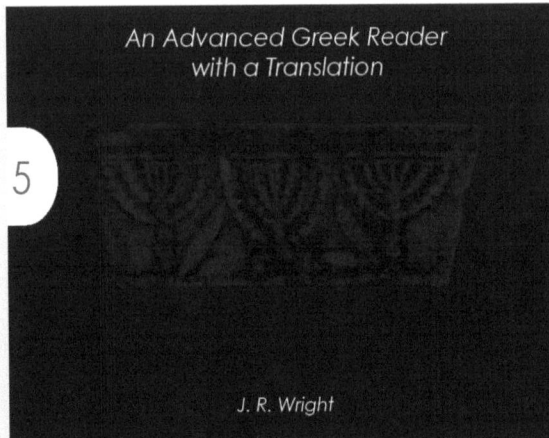

📖 LIFE OF ADAM AND EVE

This JTGR book by Jacob N. Cerone contains an introduction and the Greek texts of the Jewish Apocryphal works, *The Life of Adam and Eve* and *The Testament of Adam.*

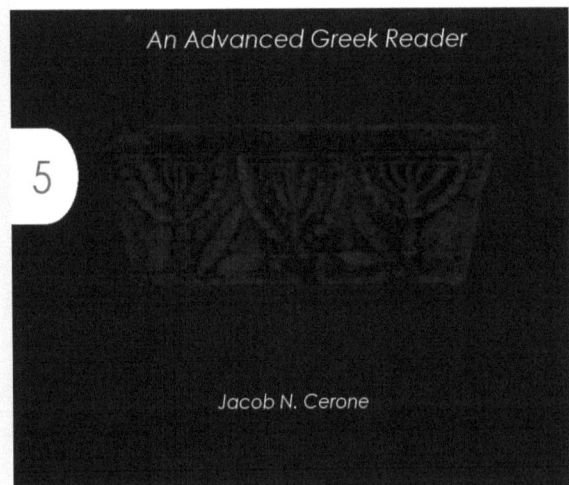

$12.99

Lives of the Prophets

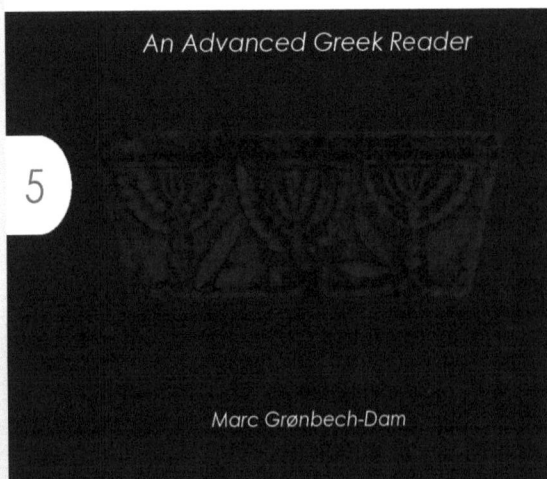

An Advanced Greek Reader

5

Marc Grønbech-Dam

1-4 BARUCH 📖

This volume by contains an introduction and the Greek texts of the Jewish Pseudepigraphal works, *1–4 Baruch.* With prepared footnotes and glosses for Greek words occurring less than thirteen times in the Greek New Testament, readers will also find translation helps and morphological helps for difficult grammatical forms.

$14.99

The Life of Adam and Eve and The Testament of Adam

An Advanced Greek Reader

5

Jacob N. Cerone

LIVES OF THE PROPHETS 📖

This particular JTGR volume contains an introduction and the Greek text of the Jewish Apocryphal work *Lives of the Prophets.* As an advanced Greek reader, included for reference is a gloss lexicon of Greek words occurring thirteen times or more in the New Testament as well as translation helps and morphological helps for grammatical forms.

Daily Devotions in Biblical Languages

D D

B L

Creation-Flood

GlossaHouse.com

DAILY DEVOTIONS IN BIBLICAL LANGUAGES 📖

This 1st volume in its series, *Daily Devotions in the Biblical Languages* (DDBL), has been specifically designed to help you maintain and grow your knowledge of the biblical languages, while practicing the disciplines of daily Scripture reading and prayer. A survey of those working on polyglot linguistics reveals that the presiding method is not to teach, so as to handle grammar, but rather teach so as to read. *Daily Devotions in the Biblical Languages* is designed to have you reading the texts every day, as this present volume provides prayers, interlinear scripture reading from Genesis and John, and high-frequency vocabulary for review.

HA'ARETS

$19.99

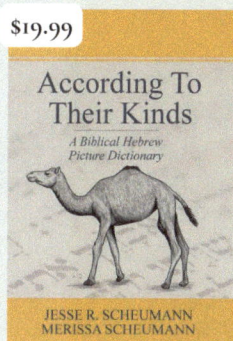

According to Their Kinds

According to Their Kinds presents all vocabulary words, paired with pictures, that occur 100 times or more in the Hebrew Bible.

$29.99

A Biblical Hebrew & Aramaic Lexicon

BHAL covers the entire biblical vocabulary, offering numerous forms to help the user to easily find a word and its grammatical forms.

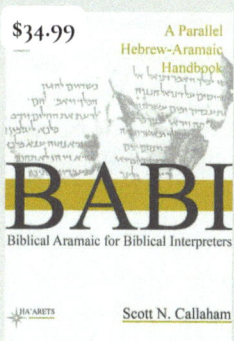

$34.99

A Biblical Aramaic Textbook

This textbook cuts an efficient path toward the interpretation of Biblical Aramaic Scripture and gives a fresh approach to learning vocabulary and grammar.

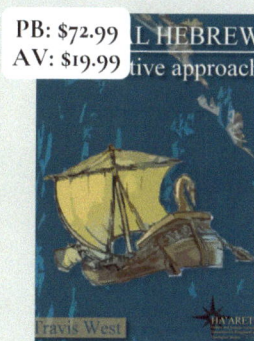

PB: $72.99
AV: $19.99

A Biblical Hebrew Textbook

This book will help you learn the original language of the Old Testament with your whole person: body, mind, and spirit, while having fun doing so.

GlossaHouse.com

$14.99

Picture Hebrew Flashcard App

This app pairs images and audio to give you an immersive learning experience, making learning Biblical Hebrew more fun.

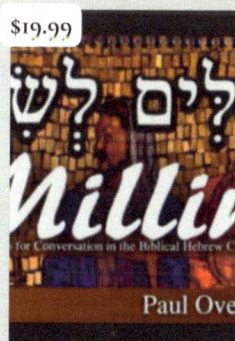

$19.99

Communication in Biblical Hebrew

The aim of this book is to give students an easy way to learn Biblical Hebrew so that they can read the Hebrew Bible with more insight.

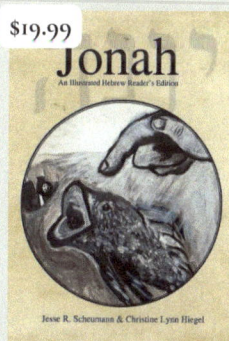

$19.99

An Illustrated Reader: Jonah

Bringing the biblical text to life with over 150 painted scenes, this book trains scholars to visualize the text of Jonah while reading.

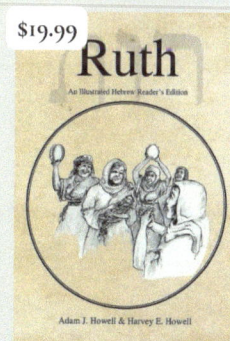

$19.99

An Illustrated Reader: Ruth

This book assists readers as they learn deeper and internalize the Hebrew language by training them to picture Ruth's text.

$19.99

$19.99

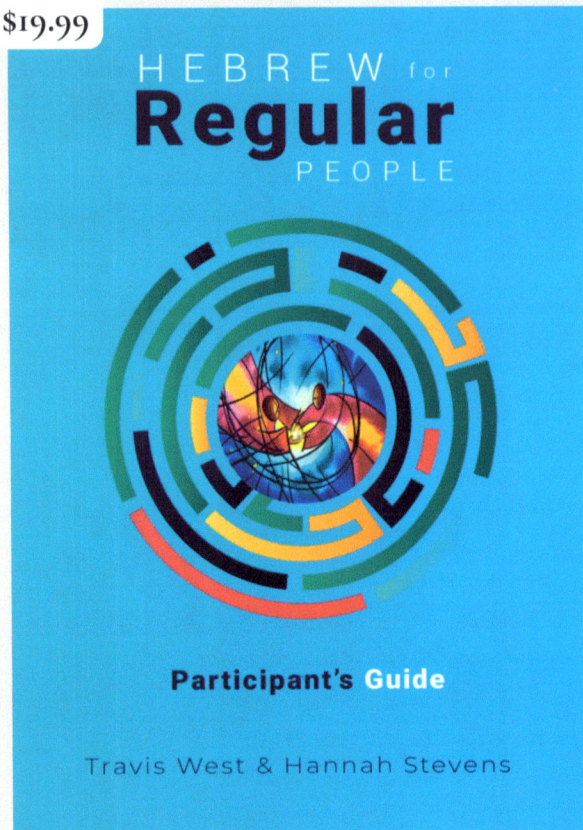

HEBREW FOR REGULAR PEOPLE: PARTICIPANT'S GUIDE

HEBREW FOR REGULAR PEOPLE: FACILITATOR GUIDE

An 8-week, class, congregational, or small group curriculum that brings aspects of the Old Testament language, culture, and practices to life for people who haven't gone to seminary but still love to learn. The Hebrew Scriptures are living and active and have the ability to breathe new life into us and mold us into the people we are created to be. And yet, not everyone experiences this transformation when engaging with the Bible in community. This study employs creative and interactive activities that encourage participants to slow down, to sit with the scriptures, and to explore practices that connect them to God, each other, and themselves. There are 2 volumes, one for participants and one for facilitators. The *Facilitator's Guide* includes lesson plans, a/v materials, Hebrew word picture art, and theological reflections while the *Participant's Guide* contains Hebrew word studies from Shema, Hebrew Songs with a Leadsheet, word picture art, and recommended reading suggestions.

ILLUSTRATED BIBLICAL TEXTS

ILLUSTRATED MATTHEW IN GREEK

This volume embeds Greek narrative, monologue, and dialogue of Matthew's Gospel within colorful illustrations, allowing the text to be contextualized in a way that words standing on the page alone simply cannot do. Along with the Greek text, a new English translation is located at the bottom of each page. These resources were created with beginning Greek student in mind, who may need help grasping Greek word meanings and understanding the significance of special constructions like direct discourse, tense usage, and participles.

Illustrated Matthew in Greek

Marc Grønbech-Dam

$34.99

Illustrated Genesis
in Hebrew בראשית

Timothy C. McNinch

GlossaHouse Illustrated Biblical Texts

Genesis in Hebrew

This resource expresses God's word and helps visual learners comprehend Genesis stories like "the creation" through detailed art.

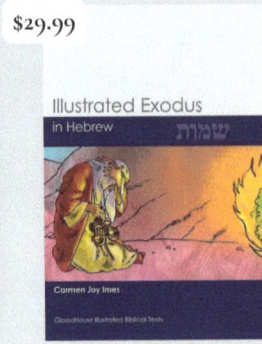

$29.99

Illustrated Exodus
in Hebrew שמות

Carmen Joy Imes

GlossaHouse Illustrated Biblical Texts

Exodus in Hebrew

Hebrew and English translations of Exodus, along with depicted stories, allow readers to practice Hebrew vocabulary and reading.

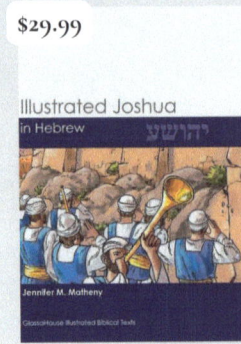

$29.99

Illustrated Joshua
in Hebrew יהושע

Jennifer M. Matheny

GlossaHouse Illustrated Biblical Texts

Joshua in Hebrew

Clear and enjoyable illustrations allow the readers to use their knowledge of ancient Hebrew and apply it to stories from Joshua in the Scripture.

$24.99

Illustrated 1 Kings
in Hebrew מלכים א

Adam J. Howell & Jonathan Ahlgren

GlossaHouse Illustrated Biblical Texts

1 Kings in Hebrew

1 Kings in its original language, embedded with full-color illustrations, is meant to help readers distinguish narrative & dialogue smoothly.

GlossaHouse.com

$26.99

Illustrated Job
in Hebrew איוב

Dominick S. Hernández

GlossaHouse Illustrated Biblical Texts

Job in Hebrew

A colorful, expansive presentation of Job written to ignite creativity & passion for learning ancient Hebrew in all students.

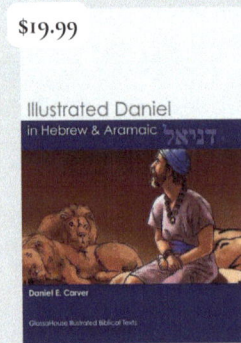

$19.99

Illustrated Daniel
in Hebrew & Aramaic דניאל

Daniel E. Carver

GlossaHouse Illustrated Biblical Texts

Daniel in Hebrew and Aramaic

Illustrated Daniel helps readers develop language skills & helps students hear and read famous stories in original languages.

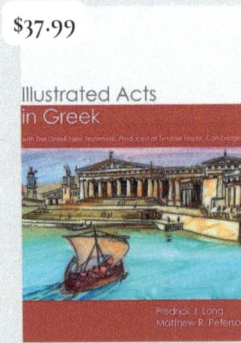

$37.99

Illustrated Acts
in Greek

with The United New Testament, Production at Tyndale House, Cambridge

Fredrick J. Long
Matthew R. Peterson

Acts in Greek

Artistic renderings of Acts shown in Greek allow the Scriptures to be contextualized and comprehended on a whole new level.

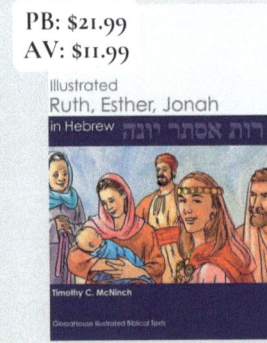

PB: $21.99
AV: $11.99

Illustrated
Ruth, Esther, Jonah
in Hebrew רות אסתר יונה

Timothy C. McNinch

GlossaHouse Illustrated Biblical Texts

Ruth, Esther, and Jonah in Hebrew

Containing illustrations of all 3 books, a helpful & engaging video file is also available to help scholars gain more experience in Hebrew.

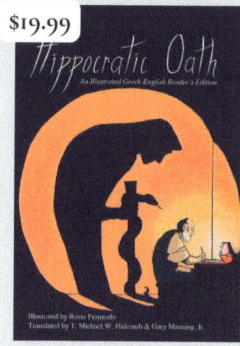

Hippocratic Oath	Daniel in Greek	Mark in Greek	John in Greek	Mark in Latin
$19.99	$29.99	$29.99	$29.99	$29.99

This book provides readers with an illustrated version of a story about the Hippocratic Oath in Koine Greek and English.

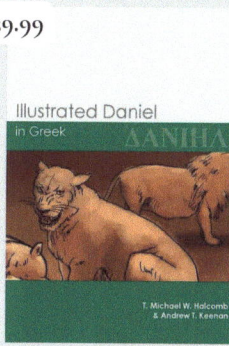

The illustration of Daniel provides visual cues for action, tension, and emotion, inviting an immersive reading experience in ancient Greek.

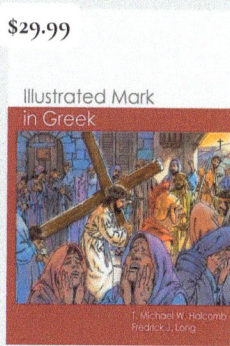

Illustrated Mark in Greek helps lead readers in learning as they explore the original text of the Gospel of Mark in an entertaining way.

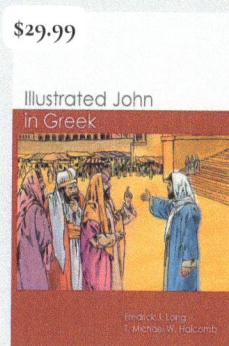

This creative work shows the Gospel of John in a new, fresh, and authentic way while engaging readers and scholars and students of all ages.

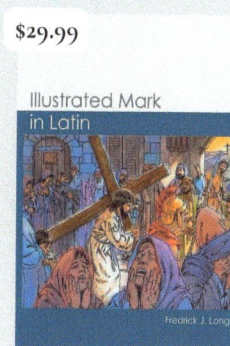

Mark Illustrated in Latin is an attractive appeal to reading Mark by a new and different means. This resource helps students apply Latin to a story.

GlossaHouse.com

DISSERTATIONS, THESES, & FESTSCHRIFTEN

$15.99

GLOSSAHOUSE
DISSERTATION
SERIES   Vol. 1

The Spirit and the Cross, Wisdom
and Communal Discernment
A Critical Exploration of 1 Corinthians 2.1-

Exploring 1 Corinthians 2

This book focuses on how Paul places emphasis on the Spirit's role in sharing the message of the cross, wisdom, and communal discernment.

$15.99

GLOSSAHOUSE
DISSERTATION
SERIES   Vol. 2

Paul the Change Agent
The Context, Aims, and Implications
of an Apostolic Innovator

Paul the Change Agent

This work, an analysis of Galatians, 1 Thessalonians, and 1 Corinthians reveals that Paul was a change agent to a culture that had long resisted change.

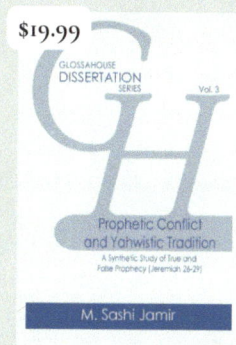

$19.99

GLOSSAHOUSE
DISSERTATION
SERIES   Vol. 3

Prophetic Conflict
and Yahwistic Tradition
A Synthetic Study of True and
False Prophecy (Jeremiah 26-29)

M. Sashi Jamir

Prophecy in Jeremiah 26-29

The aim of this dissertation is to demonstrate that ancient Israel had an adequate rubric for distinguishing true and false prophecy.

$17.99

GLOSSAHOUSE
DISSERTATION
SERIES   Vol. 4

"For You Were Bought with a Price"
Sex, Slavery, and Self-Control in a Pauline Community

Katy E. Valentine

You Were Bought with a Price

In this study, Valentine explores the notion that the Greek and Latin discourses of self-control over sexual desire undergird Paul's writings and instructions.

GlossaHouse.com

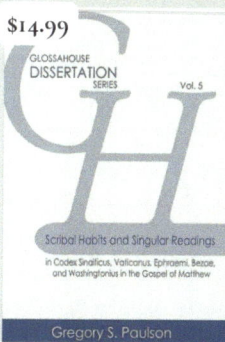

$14.99

GLOSSAHOUSE
DISSERTATION
SERIES   Vol. 5

Scribal Habits and Singular Readings
in Codex Sinaiticus, Vaticanus, Ephraemi, Bezae,
and Washingtonius in the Gospel of Matthew

Gregory S. Paulson

Scribal Habits and Singular Readings

This volume offers a text-critical portrait of scribal activity in five of the earliest extant Greek copies of Matthew.

$10.79

GLOSSAHOUSE
DISSERTATION
SERIES   Vol. 6

Rhetoric of Praise
Prayer and Persuasion in the Psalms

Ryan J. Cook

Rhetoric of Praise

This study investigates the persuasive power of the praise Psalms and how they shaped the belief and piety of ancient Israel.

$19.99

GLOSSAHOUSE
DISSERTATION
SERIES   Vol. 7

Symphony of Scriptures
An Intertextual Study of Acts 10:1-15:35

Zsolt Barta

Symphony of Scriptures

In this dissertation, Barta applies French literary theorist Gérard Genette's map of transtextuality to link points in Acts 10-15.

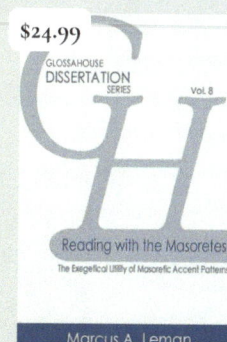

$24.99

GLOSSAHOUSE
DISSERTATION
SERIES   Vol. 8

Reading with the Masoretes
The Exegetical Utility of Masoretic Accent Patterns

Marcus A. Leman

Reading with the Masoretes

This study examines 4 ancient patterns within the book of Judges, giving overviews, examples, and evidence for each case.

$24.99

GLOSSAHOUSE DISSERTATION SERIES Vol. 9

Appropriating Ancient Authorities

Toward Understanding How Second Temple Authors Established Authority in Apocalyptic Literature

Christian A. Wilder

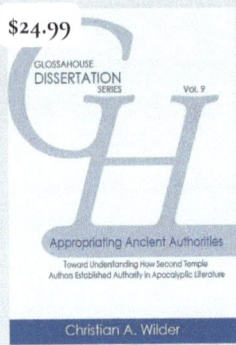

Appropriating Ancient Authority

This book explains the roots of Jewish apocalyptic literature and the political milieu of Second Temple Judaism.

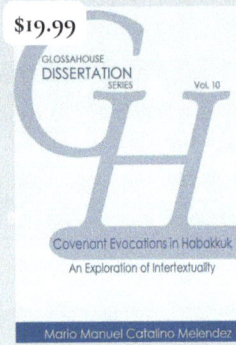

$19.99

GLOSSAHOUSE DISSERTATION SERIES Vol. 10

Covenant Evocations in Habakkuk

An Exploration of Intertextuality

Mario Manuel Catalino Melendez

Evocations in Habakkuk

In his dissertation, Melendez investigates intertextuality in the Book of Habakkuk to discover the demarcation presence of covenant.

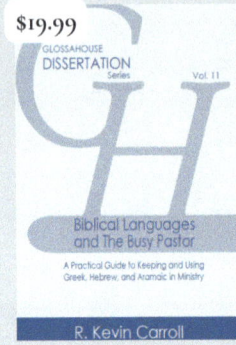

$19.99

GLOSSAHOUSE DISSERTATION Series Vol. 11

Biblical Languages and The Busy Pastor

A Practical Guide to Keeping and Using Greek, Hebrew, and Aramaic in Ministry

R. Kevin Carroll

Biblical Languages for A Busy Pastor

A scriptural, theological, historical, and practical case for why ministers should view languages as indispensable tools for ministry.

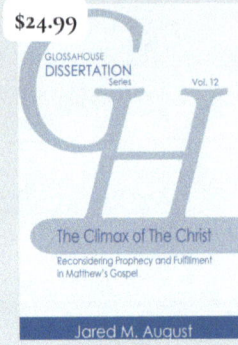

$24.99

GLOSSAHOUSE DISSERTATION Series Vol. 12

The Climax of The Christ

Reconsidering Prophecy and Fulfillment in Matthew's Gospel

Jared M. August

The Climax of The Christ

This dissertation considers Scripture citation formulas and their translations within the Gospel According to Matthew.

$24.99

GLOSSAHOUSE DISSERTATION Series Vol. 13

Middle Voice Verbs in the New Testament

Studies in Pauline Usage

Susan E. Kmetko

Middle Voice Verbs in the NT

A cutting-edge study of how to best understand Middle Voice verbs and their interpretation in Pauline Literature.

$214.99

GLOSSAHOUSE DISSERTATION SERIES Vol. 1

The Spirit and the Cross: Wisdom and Communal Discernment

GLOSSAHOUSE DISSERTATION SERIES Vol. 2

Paul the Change Agent

The Context, Aims, and Implications of an Apostolic Endeavor

GlossaHouse
Dissertation Series

GLOSSAHOUSE DISSERTATION SERIES Vol. 3

"For You Were Bought with a Price"

Katy E. Valentine

GLOSSAHOUSE DISSERTATION SERIES Vol. 5

Scribal Habits and Singular Readings

Gregory S. Paulson

GlossaHouse Dissertation Series Bundle (Vols. 1-14)

The goal of the GlossaHouse Dissertation Series is to facilitate the publication of innovative, affordable, and accessible scholarly resources, whether print or digital, that advance research in the areas of ancient and modern texts and languages. The dissertations in our series have been overseen or examined by some of the best scholars in religious academia, including Dr. Andrew T. Lincoln, Dr. Larry Hurtado, Dr. Craig Keener, Dr. Ben Witherington, Dr. Bill Arnold, Dr. David Mealand, Dr. Peter M. Head, Dr. John Cook, Dr. Steven Ybarrola, and Dr. John Oswalt. With this bundle deal, you are essentially buying 12 and getting 2 free.

$14.99   GTS 1

Jew and Gentile Reconciled:
An Exploration of the Deic Northern Tribes in Pauline Literature

Bryan E. Lewis

$15.99   GTS 2

Into the Deep
A Comparative Discourse Analysis of the Masoretic and Septuagint Versions of Jonah

Jacob N. Cerone

$19.99   GTS 3

The Biblical Hebrew Word Order Debate:
A Testing of Two Language Typologies in the Sodom Account

Jeremiah Xiufu Zuo

$19.99   GTS 4

Royal Priesthood
The New Exodus Framework of 1 Pet 1:1–2:10

Felipe A. Chamy

Jew and Gentile Reconciled

Into the Deep

Old Hebrew Word Form Debate

The New Exodus Framework

This thesis studies the narrative substructure beneath the text as it explores Paul's use of Hos 1:9–10 and 2:23 in Rom 9:24–26.

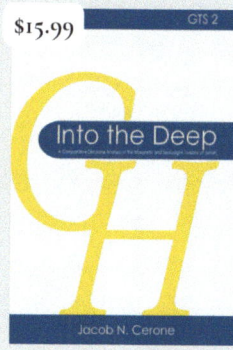

This study of Jonah utilizes discourse analysis to draw out differences between the Greek and Hebrew forms of this ancient work.

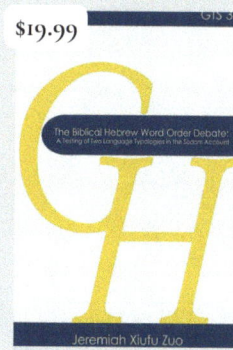

This book explores the debate over the explanatory, unique, and yet basic word order in ancient Biblical Hebrew.

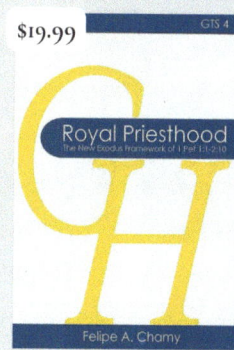

This thesis seeks to answer how the Exodus event expresses itself in 1 Peter and how it contributes to the New Testament church.

GlossaHouse Thesis Bundle (Vols. 1-4)

The goal of the GlossaHouse Thesis Series is to facilitate the publication of outstanding theses that advance research in the areas of ancient and modern texts and languages. With this bundle deal, you are essentially buying 4 and getting 1 free.

GH

GlossaHouse.com

$49.99   GTS 1

Jew and Gentile Reconciled:
Bryan E. Lewis

GTS 2
Into the Deep
Jacob N. Cerone

GlossaHouse Thesis Series Bundle (Vols. 1-4)

GTS 3
The Biblical Hebrew Word Order Debate:
A Testing of Two Language Typologies in the Sodom Account
Jeremiah Xiufu Zuo

GTS 4
Royal Priesthood
The New Exodus Framework of 1 Pet 1:1–2:10
Felipe A. Chamy

PB: $29.99
DL: $29.99

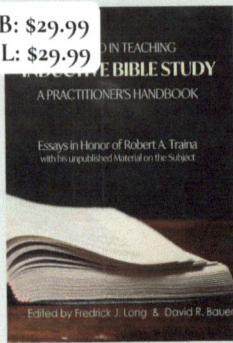

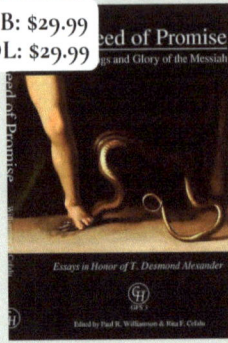

PB: $29.99
DL: $29.99

$19.99

$59.99

Inductive Bible Study

The Seed of Promise

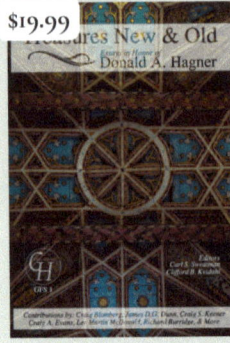

Treasures New And Old

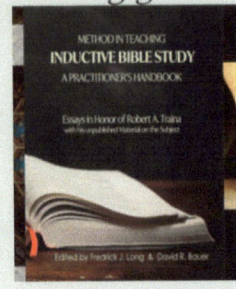

PDF Festschrift Bundle

Essays about pedagogy, church programs, discipleship, and more are all compiled into one incredible resource!

This volume is structured around the theological themes of the seed promise and the sufferings & glory of the Messiah.

Dedicated to Don Hagner, this volume explores a wide variety of topics spanning the entirety of the New Testament canon..

Over 1,200 pages of world-class exegetical, pedagogical, and theological scholarship by exegetes, educators, and theologians.

GH

GlossaHouse.com

World-Class Authors in the GH Festschrift Series

Backues, Lindy D.	Foster, Chad M.	Meenan, Alan J.
Baker, David A.	Friedeman, Matt	Millar, J. Gary
Barnett, Paul	Goldsworth, Graeme	Motyer, Stephen
Bauer, David R.	Hamilton, Jr. , James M.	Ortlund, Dane C.
Blomberg, Craig A.	Hart, Ian	Oswalt, John N.
Boyd, Rick	Hvalvik, Reidar	Petterson , Anthony R.
Brown, Jeannine K	Irons, Charles Lee	Rosner, Brian S.
Burridge, Richard A.	Johnston, Philip S.	Schenck, Kenneth L.
Byrskog, Samuel	Kiesling, Chris A.	Schliesser, Benjamin
Canon, Mark T.	Kostenberger, Andreas J.	Schreiner, Thomas R.
Cefalu, Rita F.	Kvidahl, Clifford B.	Stuhlmacher, Peter
Cockerill, Gareth Lee	Lemcio, Eugene E.	Sweatman, Carl S.
Dalrymple, Sarah	Long, Fredrick J.	Telford, William R.
Deines, Roland	Mackie, Scott D.	Traina, Robert A.
Dempster, Stephen G.	Matlock, Michael D.	Weaver, Dorothy Jean
Dendiu, John	McConville, J. Gordon	Wenham, David
Dunn, James D. G.	McDonald, Lee Martin	Williamson, Paul R.
Evans, Craig A.	McKeown, James	Quek, Eugene Wen

VARIOUS SERIES & STAND-ALONE VOLUMES

$14.50

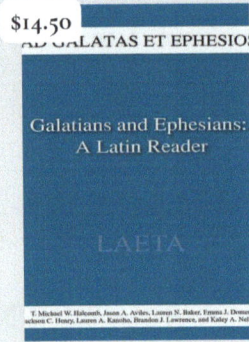

Galatians and Ephesians in Latin

This volume, engaging Galatians and Ephesians, is meant to assist beginning readers with their studying, reading, and translating of Latin.

$11.99

Speaking Latin in the Classroom

This user-friendly resource is intended to assist teachers and help learners gain a foothold in spoken Latin while having fun doing so.

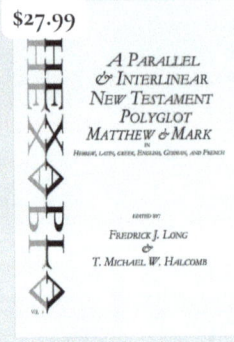

$27.99

Matthew & Mark Polyglot

This volume contains a parallel of the Gospel of Matthew and Mark, translated and written in Hebrew, German, Latin, Greek, English, and French.

$29.99

Luke-Acts Polyglot

This volume contrasts Luke and Acts in parallel formats, written in Hebrew, Latin, Greek, English, German, and French.

GlossaHouse.com

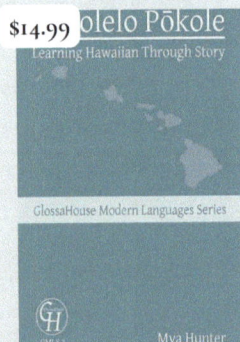

$14.99

Learning Hawaiian Through Story

Using a "Narrative Domains" approach, this volume offers an engaging entry into Hawaiian via creative storytelling.

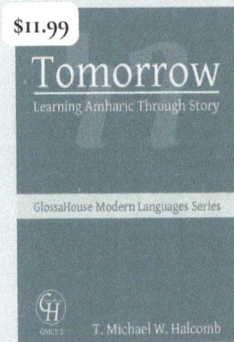

$11.99

Learning Amharic Through Story

Using a "Narrative Domains" approach, this volume strives to help readers internalize Amharic vocabulary via original storytelling.

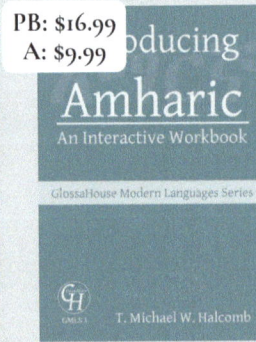

PB: $16.99
A: $9.99

Learning Amharic: A Workbook

An interactive workbook for those learning Amharic. Throughout the book, students will learn fidel, days, numbers, etc..

$7.99

Songs from the Heart - 心中音乐

This praise album contains worship songs in Chinese. The album, lyric pages, and lyric videos can all be purchased in a bundle.

$19.99

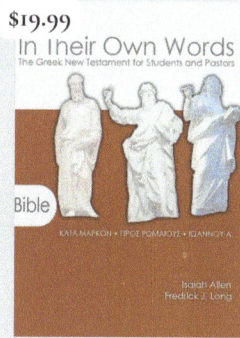

In Their Own Words

To help us develop pedagogical aims, this resource gives introductions and portions of the New Testament for study.

$15.99

Engaging Ephesians

This book explains the phenomena of the Ephesians text in a way that allows readers to work and understand it on their own.

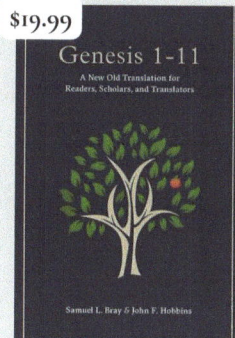

$19.99

Genesis 1-11: New Old Translation

This translation of Genesis 1-11 follows the Hebrew text closely and leaves in what many translations leave out.

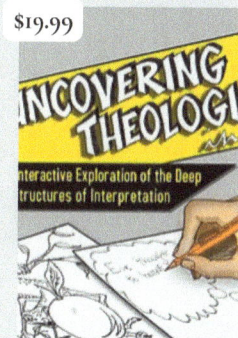

$19.99

Uncovering Theologies

This project is a creative exploration of the process of interpretation. It is an invitation to think and teach creatively.

GlossaHouse.com

$15.99

Introducing Rhetoric

Introducing Rhetoric is a fun, engaging, and sometimes challenging journey through the core elements of ancient rhetoric.

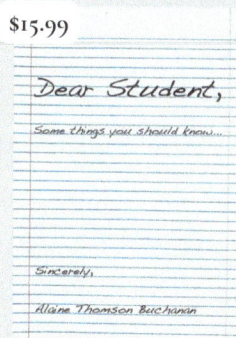

$15.99

Dear Student: Letter Compilation

This volume is a compilation of letters written from a Professor to anonymous students, covering wide variety of topics.

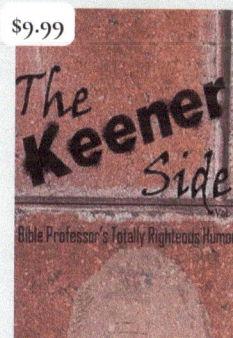

$9.99

The Keener Side: Professor's Humor

This book shows us the "keener" side of life in the academy, showing that being a scholar doesn't mean being a sourpuss.

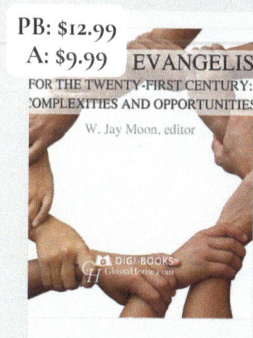

PB: $12.99
A: $9.99

Practical Evangelism

This book is designed for practitioners, giving practical approaches to evangelism that restore the good news to be new once again.

PB: $29.99
HB: $45.99

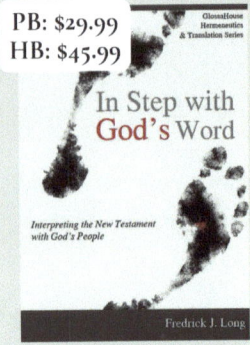

In Step With God's Word

Available in hard- and paperback style, this book presents 3 levels of studying the Scriptures for lay persons, pastors, and students.

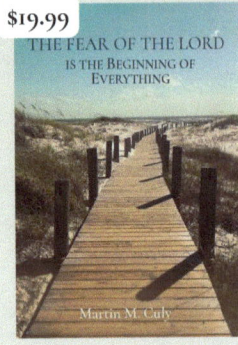

$19.99

The Fear of the Lord is the Start

This book carefully explains what the fear of the Lord is and why it is so important for our everyday lives. Readers discover it is the path to abundant life.

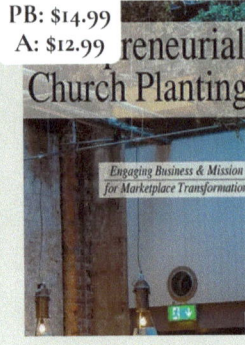

PB: $14.99
A: $12.99

Entrepreneurial Church Planting

This book explores approaches to church planting as various authors describe how entrepreneurs can create a venue for a church.

$0.99

Song of the Saints in Koine

An original song in Koine by our beloved and late friend, Dave Lloyd. We only wish he had lived long enough to finish the entire album.

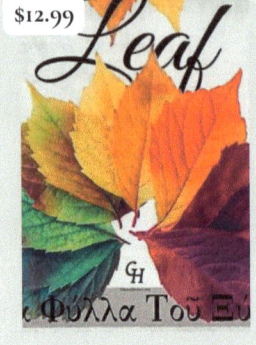

$12.99

Leaves of the Tree

Leaf, a Dutch female artist, blends her folk-acoustic style with Koine Greek Scriptures & anthems in this awesome album.

GlossaHouse.com

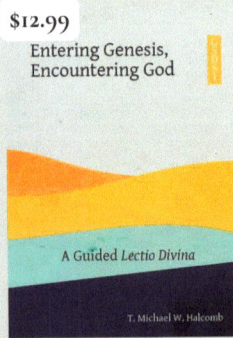

$12.99

Entering Genesis, Encountering God

This book is written in the tradition of lectio divina, encouraging readers to enter Genesis with the expectation of encountering God there.

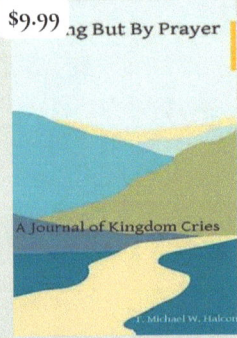

$9.99

Nothing But By Prayer: Journal 1

Halcomb invites readers into his prayer journal, hoping they will join him in prayer and be inspired to write their own prayers.

$9.99

Intentional Living: Journal 2

In his second prayer journal, Halcomb invites readers to join him in prayer, recycle his prayers, and create their own prayers.

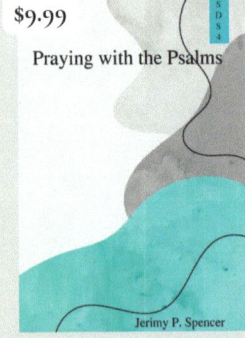

$9.99

Praying with the Psalms

Jerimy Spencer offers a daily reflection on specific verses from each of the 150 Psalms. Readers will love this creative work.

GlossaHouse.com Gift Card

You can give the gift of learning to anyone around the world with this e-gift card of your choice amount, redeemable at GlossaHouse.com.

Aleph With Beth: Learn Hebrew!

Andrew and Bethany Case are scholars, fulfilling their calling to teach biblical Hebrew as they create free, high-quality resources for anyone!

GlossaHouse's ProveText Podcast

6 days of the week, Dr. T. Michael W. Halcomb and Dr. Fredrick J. Long release an episode of their podcast, exploring Scripture & everything related to it.

The Bridge Church Podcast

Listen or watch the weekly Sunday sermons from Pastor Michael Halcomb, who currently pastors The Bridge Church on Oahu, Hawai'i.

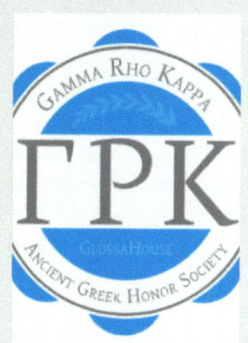

Gamma Rho Kappa

Gamma Rho Kappa is an international Greek Honor Society that recognizes outstanding achievement in the study of Ancient Greek.

GlossaHouse.com

www.ingramcontent.com/pod-product-compliance
Lightning Source LLC
Chambersburg PA
CBHW040022050426
42452CB00002B/89